Nature Sings—
and so do we

Poems
by
Paul Grayson

Nature Sings

Sonnet

When I have ceased to move, I shall not die,
As long as stands a rock upon a hill;

The birds will give me wings and I will fly,
I will get leaves and trunk, I will stand still.

I shall move panther-like through hungry spaces,
I shall be flower, moss, and grass, and tree,

I shall be integrated with a thousand races
That ever were and ever hope to be.

I shall drop from the clouds as falling rain,
I shall course to the rivers down the brooks,

I shall be merciless, yet merciful, and gain
A comprehension in a thousand looks.

I know when I have gone I shall not die ----
As long as there is sea or earth or sky.

P. Grayson

Preface

I have always loved being outdoors with the wonders of nature; its plants and trees, its flowers and weeds. I hope you enjoy these morsels, which I pen to voice what I hear and see.

I dedicate this book to my family and friends, and especially the two loves of my life: Barbara and Lucia.

I thank my many poetry friends, Judith McCombs for her constant encouragement, Barbara O'Donnell for retyping much of my manuscript, Maritza Rivera for reviewing the initial draft and helping with its organization, and fellow poet and friend, Richard Epstein, who undertook this effort and made it happen.

Note: All photographs without attribution were obtained and provided by my design team.

Photograph by
Paul Grayson.

Contents

We, the Weeds

We are the weeds you deprecate,
We are the weeds you love to hate,
We spoil the green of your lawns
With:

> the gold of the bitter sorrel.
> the blue of the speedwell.
> r o s e of the pimpernel.
> and pink of the Deptford.

We festoon, we decorate, we embroider
The cracks in your sidewalks,
The space between old railroad ties,
And edges of dusty gravel paths,

> We, the lambs-quarters,
> We, milky lowly spurge
> We, the foxtail grass
> We, the pigweed and ragweed and knotweed,
> who bring the snuffling season.

You may, for moments, escape from us
By running off to the tall timber,
Or to splash the ocean's salt,
or to glide in a mile-long floating casino
into Caribbean ports;
But when, at last, you reappear,
We shall be here,
We . .

> Shall . .
> Be. .
> Here.

August 14, 2008

1

November Garden

We can't go to the plot again?
      To work the dirt
      And picnic in the sun,
      To pluck the weeds
      And cut the black-eyed susan?
No more tomatoes we can take,
No gleaming pepper we can crop,
And no more sand to spread and rake?
      And straw to scatter –
      Is that a finished matter?
We live within earth's cycle
      And the rolling seasons eventually will get
Us once more to the planting
      And the digging and the dirt and the sweat.
And while a thunderstorm may glower,
We'll be soaping in the shower.

December 2000

Sticks

Forty years ago, the saplings on the grounds shed leaves,
     And in the fall
     We raked them—that was all.
Mature big trees they are today,
And they have grown in every way.
     And after storms and thunder pass,
     Dead sticks and twigs bestrew the grass.
Trees have a way of growing old
     Much different from humankind;
To grow in strength while growing old
     Is something that I would not mind …
--That's a very personal statement, of course,
But, on viewing the woody wreckage on the ground,
I am reminded
That what I really meant to say
(Before I was seduced by the clink of rhyming)
Is simply this:
     Growth entails loss;
     And we're not that much different
          from trees after all.

Autumn Galaxy:
Created by the author
from maple seed pods
(samaras).

3

Leaves

I sallied forth with rake in hand
To clear the leaves from off my land,
Until their colors I did see,
Mauve and magenta, ivory,
Green and golden, lemon, tan,
Orange bright and orange wan,
Chartreuse, deep brown, vermillion.
I had to gaze at every one –
That's why the job is still not done.

November 1999

A Leaf's Story

Books are so full these days
Of little what-have-yous that tried and tried and made it.
That is sanctimonious cant:
I tried and tried and couldn't make it.
Look, here I am,
Stretched on the ground,
A leaf like all other leaves.
We all tried to stay,
God knows I tried;
I was down to one delicate thread,
That was all that connected me.
I spun around and around in the wind
At the end of that thread,
Holding my breath and trying, trying,
It was no use.
As a cloud moved across the sun,
Distracting me,
A sudden extra gust caught me unawares,
And I went sailing.
That might have looked exhilarating to you,
But I had a sinking feeling,
And now, here I am,
Stretched on the ground like all the others.
God knows what will become of me …
Mulch?

Winter Lines to a Leafless Tree

Take a break, pal,
      Rest, and take it easy;
Don't do anything for a while,
      Now the weather's turned so freezy.

You've had an exciting spring,
      And wearying summer,
An exhausting fall,
      And now the weather's come a bummer.

Your twigs lengthened,
      Your leaves expanded.
Your flowers opened,
      Your seeds have sprouted where the wind has landed.

You've gone through the routine,
      You've done the drill,
So now's the time:
      Do nothing, Nada, Nil.

November 22, 2006

Winter Rain Drops:
Created by the author
from hanger wire and
parts of a cottage
cheese carton.

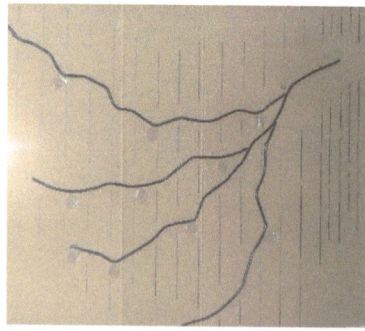

Two Little Boys

So there were these two little boys
Standing under this big tree,
Looking up at its brown and twisted leaves
And I couldn't help but hope
That they were wondering,
Not how to get their pet cat down,
Not how to dislodge a stuck football,
But why is this tree covered in brown leaves
When all the others are green?

October 17, 2005

The Rake and the Shovel

Caring for a house,
Caring for the grounds,
There was a time for shoveling
And a time for raking;
A time for putting
And a time for taking.
Winter meant snow and shoveling,
And after the snow,
Put the shovel away.
Summer meant grass and leaves and
raking,
And after the leaves,
Put the rake away.

But the snow comes so soon after the leaves,
And the leaves come so soon after the snow,
That putting and taking cannot keep up:
The rake and the shovel should stand side by side
outside the house,
together now,
all year round.

October 8, 1999

My Dogwood Tree

I shall sit under my dogwood tree
And read,
And muse,
And doze,
And let the fitful breeze,
Half-warm, half-cool,
Flow over me.
I shall no longer be mister wise-acre,
Mister master of knowledge,
Mister dancer, prancing on his tight rope.
Mister gymmaster lover, master of strange moves,
Mister artist and poet, cousin to the graces.
Mister artificer and fix-it child of Hephaestus.

I shall sit under my dogwood tree,
And the leaves shall reach down
And try to caress me.

July 22, 2001

The Goldenrod and the Frost

It's August now. The goldenrod flaunts yellow in the fields,
But the chill of the killing frosts approaches.
This is the time of year the goldenrod stands tall
And waves a memory of my lost father.

I well remember that autumn – how it was:
This flower, this plant – eager, then as now, to live and bloom –
Thrust up and raised its fingers out
Through the tall grasses,
Through the cool mornings, each one cooler,
And the warm afternoons, each less warm.
Bee and wasp and moth hummed and tumbled
On the flowery mass,
And shiny beetle and iridescent fly came there to feed . . . .

The morning the first frost came on the world,
The goldenrod was burned with cold and trembled.
That afternoon, the sweet sun warmed
The twisted leaves and shrunken buds;
Thus encouraged and emboldened,
New flowering heads emerged and yellow gleamed
And a low sound from the goldenrod was heard,
The number of its visitors reduced,
And the rest subdued . . . .

So did the year's heat cycle roll:
Pitiless and keen, the frost struck hard again the following night;
Once more the goldenrod fought back,
The sun helping the yellow open through the brown,
The seared leaves curling, twisting, falling,
The almost quiet plant stiff and tall;
Again, again, the frost, the frost –
Brave goldenrod! It blooms! It fights! It lives! . . . .

It died.
The cloudy cold of day followed a chilling night:
It was too much –

The cycle of life cannot be long arrested –
On it rolled . . .

Risen from seed or rhizome in the earth,
Last year's goldenrod still standing now,
Knows in its time it fed its rhizome.
Grew and threw its seed;
And now it sees this year's glow and glitter all around it,
Hears a newer hum and tumble,
And knows the frost's triumph
Is but temporary.

Ode to Every Autumn

I've marveled at the autumn
      For seventy years and more,
And I will always feel the same
If I live another score.

I treasured as a youngster,
      I wonder at it still;
I revel in the glory of the splendor of the autumn,
      And I always will.

And if, next year, I feel the urge
      To re-express my bliss,
I'll simply reach into my files—
      And read from this.

November 8, 2002

Autumn in a Gated Community

On our five-foot fig tree,
There are exactly four leaves left,
Lobed just like the ones on
       male Greek statues.
Ours are yellow,
Surrounded by sharp pointed green buds
Impatient for the spring.
But the Grounds Committee has ruled
"No deciduous fruit-bearing trees may
      be planted"
(They just discovered ours).
So we reap the harvest:
A tropical tree too far north.

November 1, 2012

While Making Breakfast

I'm making my breakfast. It's late October.
But I still eye the red humming bird feeder
Clinging outside the dining room window
What a strike! -- if a hummer showed up--
The buzz of its wings twinkling in the light!
As I pour the cereal and slice the grapes into my bowl,
I also keep a wary eye for a repeat
Of yesterday's domestic tsunami of ants,
Sweeping an ant from behind the bread board.
Location, location, location, they say:
It all depends where the wildlife is.

October 3, 2011

Spring from an Ancient Hande

Now dothe the greene leaf
Peek from the out the budd,
And the oak's large limbs be shadowed
And hidden,
And the winter's architecture blurred
By the unresting motion of the aire.
Now the delicate branches of the maple
be swathed in gaudy greenery
so they become invisible,
pouring they're prodigal pollen
To the recipient winde.
How unlike each maple
Is every other maple
(Red, sugar, mountain, silver, sycamore);
How unlike each oak,
Is every other oak
(Red, white, scrub, rubra, alba, macrocarpa).
The blackness of winter –
Darkness on white –
there is where true beauty lies,
Flaunting itself against the lowering skies.

April 2015

Spring Morning

Doddering old fool—
And I guess I qualify on all three counts.
In the cool of the spring and the shade of the wood,
And the sun on the bank
Facing the river and sprawled on the bank
Twitters and quacks and calls,
Waiting for something to arrive.
When the kingfisher flew downstream,
Something arrived and I roused.
By a pondish swale, the park people
Had kindly planted yellow and blue iris;
Nearby skunk cabbage luxuriously lolled,
(How do these plants manage to find those wet places?
When they rarely produce flowers?)
Pollywogs rested on the muddy bottom
Frogs splashed headlong to join them.
Into the wood where dry leaves rested on the rotting,
Up and down searching for the little orchid.
What was its name? Epipactis? Sullivantii?
No, no, the one called Rattlesnake Plantain.
Goodyera that's it. Up and down,
I can't believe that somewhere in this wood
There isn't a small patch of it.
Back and forth it must be here somewhere. . .
Well then, next time.
Doddering old fool!

May 24, 2006

A Plea to the Peas in the Plot

Oh little peas, raise your tender heads,
Rise out of the soil from your wintry bed;
      Send out your tendrils and climb the rods
      So that we can reap your nutritious pods.
          Grow green and tall,
            May your harvest be ample,
          And set for the others
            An abounding example.

May 4, 2001

The Madness of Life

So this is Spring --- again,
And the natural world pulsates,
Striving in its mad unreasoning way
To keep the germ plasm flowing.
Spring peeper males advertise that they're available,
Clouds of samaras swirl from the maples,
Wren couples investigate every unlikely
         nesting site,
While teen-agers stuff themselves
         into their tightest fitting jeans,
And wasp pupae stir in their ceramic cells
         and gnaw their way to freedom and fulfillment.
This lavish expenditure of energy,
Gametes contending and combining furiously with each other.
Live, to propagate!
Propagate, to live!

May 14, 2007

The Sycamore of Anxiety

I used to get sick with anxiety
Every year at this time of the Spring:
The oaks had hung their green tassels,
And high in the tulip trees
Big bold flowers stared back at the sun.
But the gleaming sycamore - - -
    the one behind our little shopping center - - -
Nothing, no sign of life, nothing.
Was it dead? Was it merely late? Would it leaf? . . .
At last its leaves and bally flowers came forth,
And all was well (at least for another year) . . .
And so I learned to trust nature and the tree
And not get bent out of shape - -
It always leafed, it always will, be reassured.
But we know what can happen, don't we,
When we start taking things for granted.

I Know a Bank

There was a bank in the woods I knew
In days long gone where the bloodroots grew,
Alone in the dead leaves, just exposed,
Facing the rumble of the road,
Their petals white and few and frail
Barely surviving by the trail.
For merely a minute in the Spring
Was the bloodroot's time for flowering.
No other flower, no other leaf,
It was bloodroot's time so swift, so brief;
At the foot of the gaunt and sunlit tree,
For companion a titmouse and chickadee.
And the years have passed and still I know
The way to the bank where the bloodroots grow.

March 30, 2008

Cricket

Humpback bouncing
  On the basement floor,
You did not come here
  To explore.

I swear I will not
  Chase or chide,
If this is where
  You wish to hide.

A basement warm,
  A haven dry,
Almost protected
  From a prying eye

The late year's frost
  You wish to shun,
Although your days
  Are almost run;

Are almost run,
  Be dry or wet,
The end's the same
  And yet, and yet –
I give you
  My profound regret.

December 1, 1999

Sally in the Year of ...

Someone told me two or three years ago
It was the Year of the Tiger.
Well, this year is the year of the Cicada,
Right?
But it's kind of my year too,
Because I am seventeen this year,
Just like them.
I came out of the darkness seventeen years ago,
The same year they went into it.
Each of us has been growing in our own way:
There's only one of me
And so many of them,
Making such a holler,
Climbing up,
Then throwing themselves down,
Now they have done what they were born to do.
I shall go on and see their children
When I'm thirty-four.
But for now, I feel mournful
And step carefully around their dark and quiet bodies.

June 8, 2004

A Field Guide to (Some of) the Birds of America

Let's get this straight:
    There's nothing darling
        about a starling;
And a sparrow
        does not fly like an arrow.
But it's true that an eagle
Has more than one fliegel.
And the view's not quite complete
When you're in the catbird's seat.

And by the way, un-a propos,
It's crows that caw and cocks that crow.

The weird songs of a mocker
Do not mean he's off his rocker.

It's not true that the flicker
Is unduly fond of liquor;

It is really the sapsucker
That becomes a little shicker.

And don't look for larks
In American parks.

And as for the robin
Don't count on his bobbin'
He may feel more like jogging'.

And hawks, when they fly,
Do not circle the sky.

Give respect to the raven--
For he's quite a maven.

And the light of the moon
Will show you a loon.

One swallow maketh not a spring,
But summer comes beneath its wing.

Watch turkey vultures with misgiving,
Don't carve them up for your Thanksgiving.

Oh see the pigeons strut and coo;
Beware, they may have avian flu.

Try to forget the things you've heard:
A bird is a bird is just a bird.

March 31, 2003

Wrens

We had a visit
      From a wren,
It brought a mate when it
      came back again.

And they had weeds to bring
      And eggs to lay,
But then they vanished
      One night? One day?
Next year perhaps
      They'll come to stay.

The spring will come
      We hope they're here,
Their songs to sing,
      Their chicks to rear.
We hope the wrens
      will reappear.

September 18, 2007

Martins

The dart and twitter of these purple martins
The sweep of their wings across this glassy pool,
Sweeps me back years--no, decades--
To when I saw them in my boyhood,
Marshalling their ranks in the Septembers,
Flocking and resting,
Wheeling and testing,
Spreading like an inky blot across the sky,
To suddenly converge and settle
On the wires stretched across the street.
Murmuring and chirping,
Descending and swirling,
Preparing for the great day, as of old,
When our forefathers asked
"Where have all the swallows gone?"
And the wise men answered:
"They plunge into the mud which,
When loosened from winter's icy grip,
Releases them, and they return to us.
It's that simple!"

July 26, 2009

A Nest in the Sukkah

Sparrows are collecting dry weeds, grass stalks, twig fragments
In their annual rites of spring—
Building a nest in the Sukkah
That hugs the synagogue wall.
They are perfectly committed to the injunction:
Your booth shall be such
That you shall see
The sky of heaven above you through the spaces.

April 2016

A Stitch in the Current of Time

In a little space of bare ground
Chattering sparrows dust themselves
Fluttering up little clouds of dust
To rid mites from their feathers.

Above the dust is a bulge in the wall
And the bulge contains the ark,
And the ark contains the Torah.

And if the sun beats hard enough upon the wall
And if the rain beats hard enough upon the wall
So that it gives way,
Smothering the dusty sparrows,
It will be very hard on the sparrows,
To say nothing about the Torah.

April 21, 2007

The Gift of Fruit

This jar of stewed fruit my dear friend has given me.
The gift was unexpected,
And the fruit's flavor is exceptional.
Cloudy with white mold.
After many days in the refrigerator,
It's still delicious,
And I will not throw it out.
In this way, I shall honor the giver
And the impulse that gave it to me.

Picnic, Colorado Mountain Valley

In the midst of this great and arid plain,
Where neither soil nor water smile on growth
Yet where the land is decked with the lupine's purple,
The scarlet gilia, the sunflowers' gold, and harebell's delicate blue,
We built a fire, roasted meat and potatoes
In a pine tree's breezy shade,
While distant thunder thumped up from
the surrounding mountains.
Golden, green and red, splotches of lichen,
Decorated the rose-red boulders that we sat on,
And sagebrush, that gray eminence,
Reigned over all imperturbably.

Ignorance is the Child of Conviction*

God made you,
Noah saved you, he said,
Gazing down at the remains of a gopher
(Probably Geomys bursarius, he mused),
Bloody at the edge of the prairie road that disappeared
       over the next rise.
A keen observer, he noted there were many black
       spots along the sides
Of this creature here in Carroll County,
The bluestem grass and sunflowers nodding above him.
In the Dakotas, he knew—a funny thing:
Gophers had no spots.
And in between, in Iowa, even more interesting:
Gophers had a few faint spots.
God made them that way, he said reverently,
And plucked a stone from his right shoe.

*With equal justification, Louise Gluck has it: "Ignorance wills
something imagined which it believes exists." –From "A Myth
of Innocence" in Averno, Farrar Strauss-Giroux, 2006.

September 23, 2006

The Beach, Oostburg

Out sang the plaintive pewee's mourning calls
To wail the sun's rays sluicing down the halls
Of Nature's high-borne palace as, far-sent,
The night's dark-blue and violet palls were rent
And stretched apart. Far bent the quivering heaps
Of clouds, extended, still, above the deeps
As, shifting-colored by the spreading light,
Above them leaped the sun. Beneath its flight
Bright-flecked sun-sparkled waters gave a shout
And danced three times as high to see the rout
Of night. The pewee's pout was answered now:
An ovenbird beneath a maple bough
Gave tongue vociferously; a crow called loud;
A killdeer upward sprang; and yet a crowd
Of myriad voices, elusive and unknown,
Bowed unseen to the ears; silver high-flown,
A sea-gull wheeled and screamed a shriller note, --
Blown with the wind he spied a fisher's boat
And floated thence.

Down on the cream-brown beach,
In all directions far as eyes could reach,
Stretched the four parts of which our world was made,
Each separate and distinct: the part of shade,
The green, close-knitted wood; and then the sky
Where play the sunlight and the stars, where fly
The bird-wings and the rains; the changeful lake,
Beneath which lie the spirits which must slake
Unnatural thirsts with blood, --genii that churn
And quake the waters with a raging burn,
Imps that turn Heaven to avenging Hell,
Laughing without reason – but to break the spell,

Turn Hell about and soothe it into Heaven,
Making all well, gentle where they have striven—
This was the third part of our world; the last—
It was the beach, firm-bound and riven fast
Between the blast-tormented quickened foam
And the green lands where Pan has made his home
Beneath the oak among the birch and pine,
In Nature's womb of moss and fern and vine
Where thrashers flit their tails and thrushes sing,
And blue hare-bells incline their heads to fling
Their color toward a blue and purple cloud
High o'er the wood.

Close by, deep blue and proud,
The torn waves of the lake rolled toward the shore
And glowed as if with fire, with still more
Of brightness underneath than shone above.
Before the horizon, cones of color drove
Harmonious lanes of purple, green, and blue,
Blending, as if in love with all the peaceful view.
So, with kind breezes and a gentle sun
Time passed for us upon its daily run,
And day which had begun – or so it seemed –
Drew fast to closing. Though the red sun beamed,
He shuddered as he watched the mad approach
Of Night's swift-moving blue and silver coach
That flew out from the east, whose coursing steeds
Encroached upon and swept the swollen meads
Above. And Night let hang the trailing reins
And slackened speed.

Now silken fiery lanes
Of amber circled through the western sky
And chains of faery gossamer gradually

33

Spun through the highest reaches. In the east,
Low clouds were somber at the dazzling feast
Of light and color; now they seemed more fair—
A cloud moved through the upper hyaline air,
And bared them letting fall a flood of light!
Now a most glorious and noble sight
Was blazoned on our eyes – of color bold,
Red-orange and deep purple. But to behold
Was to exclaim and to compare the thing:
Piles of warm snow folded, and coloring
With deep blushes, while gathering at the base,
Deep thrilling shadows wrapped about the face;
Far distant mountain ranges capped with snow
Gilded and shadowed tenderly; next, there below,
The deepening violet, like a row of trees,
Outlined in silhouette with wavy ease
A sylvan backdrop for this monstrous play:
Above were more scenes for the end of day
Through which were glimpses of more acts;
and then a sky-line set
Low in the sky in dusky silhouette—
This too the low clouds seemed, while higher still,
The orange massy clouds loomed like a giant's will …
The gods sat on Olympus at that hour –
This was the climax, this the noble flower
Of all that long day's myriad loveliness:
The flower and moss, the tree, the hidden nest
Had all existed, waiting but for this,
This touch of beauty like a goddess' kiss; --
And so we gazed, consumed, our very souls
Shivering, as when deep thunder rolls
And crashes …

The last of color now was gone,
The sun had had his moments and was done;
And Night, her garments spreading through the air
Drove on, robing the sky left blue and bare
At the sun's fall, with a blue stuff so clear,
So fair and dainty, and so light and sheer,
That pale light points pricked through the shaded sky.
Later the whip-poor-will would sing his cry,

But now the wind hung silently above the hill—
Tongues their harsh clangor hushed, for now the thrill
Of sweeping silence floated graciously
Upon the world. And every standing tree
Became a column or a pyramid
Or leafy arm, outlined in black amid
His fellows, on the sky. Darker, still darker, sank
The world; and deeper, still deeper, all life drank
The sacred dew of rest within the forest's flow …
While to the waves, the moon has lent its glow,
It and the stars remain, and dusky sleep,
And night, relaxed and cool, intense and deep.

July 19, 1935

At the Rehab Center

In this garden, in the courtyard
of the rehab center, there be blue jays here;
It was an unsubstantiated hypothesis,
but now confirmed. One flared
his blue just now in the young Gleditsia.
And the Buddleya bush is an attraction
to the swallowtail butterfly--
we nailed that down three days running.
A fount of wisdom at age 97?
More like a weak stream of self-pity.
I ran away from the physical therapist,
hearing her gasping "Wait for me!"
The August days are dominated by the three H's
(haze, heat and humidity) as the heat index
soars above 100, while the 2016 Olympic games
play out in Rio.

August 14, 2016

Six Whimsies

1. The Exile

Every year, come January,
Our Camellia bush starts to put out
One lush white flower after another.
I warn it:
   --don't be in such a hurry,
   --heavy wet snows may yet arrive.
It thinks it's growing down in Charleston,
Surrounded by live oaks and Spanish moss.
It's no use talking,
There's no arguing with a homesick Camellia.

2. On the Roofs

On the supermarket's roof
   Ring-billed gulls are clustered,
They await the throw-out of
   Produce that cannot pass muster.

The bank next door has on its roof
   More gulls in number myriad;
Perhaps they think the bank will scrap
   Old worn-out money going bad.

3. Through the Window

A squirrel racing up and through
The twigs and branches--
Why the urgency, little brother?
And the twigs shaking and swaying
As if a great gust of wind were passing through:
What a tremendous fuss to be kicked up
By such a little fellow!

4. That Pass in the Night

When the recycling truck that collects paper
Crosses the path
Of the car delivering the morning newspaper,
I guess we're kind of lucky
That one doesn't say to the other,
Wouldn't it be more efficient
If we just cut out the middle man?

5. An Asian Elephant Ponders his Mahout

He pricks me on one side and I turn.
He jabs the other side and I reverse.
What is there in me
That puts up with this nonsense?
Why didn't I stamp my foot a long time ago,
And blot him out?
What is there in me?
That little monkey perched on my back,
Thinking how he lords it over me,
How did I get to be this way?
Is there something going on here
That I don't understand?

6. An Ornithological Commentary

Great black crows lounge through our neighborhood,
Enjoying urban amenities not available out in the sticks.
Great white seagulls stalk the nearby malls,
From which they launch reconnoitering overflights.
Perhaps, soon, they too shall come to live among us.
When they do, I am expecting
That the white birds and the black
Will peacefully and amicably . . . .
    share the garbage.

The Geese of Leisure World

The packed snow melting
The old folks walk the paths again
Carefully, they stay off the grass,
Peppered with thumb -sized droppings
      of the geese.
Years ago, management bequeathed to them the job
of lawn control,
And now they make it through the winter
on handfuls of corn close sprinkled by the pond.
In a few weeks honking sounds will
      echo overhead,
And our fat geese will simply bob their heads and search for corn.
"Who's making all that clatter in the sky?
Why are they calling (up, come up and fly?)"
Why not turn those geese into
      paté' de fois gras,
And start over?

February 13, 2000